MOLLY ENCHANTS HER WORLD

A RETURN TO LOVE

MOLLY
BOOK TWO

ANNA CAMILLA KUPKA

BUTTERFLY PUBLISHING

Butterfly Publishing – Anna Camilla Kupka
Zürich, Switzerland
Text: Anna Camilla Kupka
Illustrations: Carole Isler
Editor: Ursula Tanneberger
Translations: Doreen Zeitvogel

Molly is happily pedaling along the winding path, her hair blowing in the wind as she savors the warmth of the air on her skin. The sun is tickling her with its rays, and Molly begins to think of the rich and colorful inner world she just got to know a few weeks ago, a world as varied as this beautiful summer's day. Above all, she realizes now that her innermost core is nothing other than pure love. Since she found this out, she feels as if she has been reborn, and she sees herself and the world in a new light.

What fascinates Molly most of all is that everything in her outward life has somehow also changed. It's as though her new self-confidence is literally written on her forehead for all to see at a glance. For since that time, everyone has been different towards her—kinder. The girls who always teased her have held back, and her brother is now no longer such a pest.

She's also doing better in school because she's more relaxed about how she sees things, and she can take them seriously without getting overwhelmed. She now takes things one at a time and in this way completes them all—even her homework, which before seemed almost impossible. Now she knows that what we imagine a thing to be is often worse than the thing itself.

Anyhow, she knows a lot more than before. And the others are noticing, too, although they don't know the real reason behind it. Her mother, for instance, keeps looking at her in amazement lately, which makes Molly grin. After her visit to her inner world, she almost feels like a wise, old lady—as if she herself could tell her mother a thing or two about life. But she doesn't. Besides, her mother might not understand.

And so, lost in thought, Molly finally arrives at her favorite spot, a leisurely babbling brook that winds its way through the green grasses and flowering meadows. Here, she's undisturbed and free and close to the natural world. The bees are buzzing around her, and everywhere there's chirping and humming as summer makes itself not only felt and seen but heard. A wonderful peace and lulling calm prevail. Molly sets her bike to the side, rolls up her pants, and dangles her feet in the cool stream. Then she lies on her back and watches the clouds go by.

Her thoughts shift slowly to Brittany, who is in the same class and has always tried to make life difficult for Molly. Things have gotten better now, and at least Brittany doesn't bother her anymore, but Molly doesn't understand why this girl is still so cold and distant. She thinks they could actually get along quite well, but Brittany is too standoffish. And Molly has too much pride to try to be chummy.

Before, Brittany's behavior had hurt Molly, and she was even afraid to go to school sometimes. She sees things differently now since her journey to her true nature, but she still wishes she could understand what's going on in a person like Brittany, what she's thinking and feeling. She wonders if she feels how Molly did before she got to know her innermost being. Back then, she often felt confused, and a lot of things didn't make sense. Does Brittany maybe feel the same way, and is that why she's always so cold and seemingly unhappy?

Interesting question, thinks Molly. But she doesn't have an answer. After all, she can't look inside other people. Which is actually too bad, because it would be interesting to know what it looks like inside other people.... That was her last thought before an deafening noise rang out within her.

Molly jumps. *What's going on here?* A loud male voice is yelling at her and telling her what to do. She can only make out bits and pieces of words:

"Come on!" "When will you finally ...?" "Haven't I said it a thousand times ...?" "You have to ..." "Don't be so stupid ...."

Molly can feel a sense of panic spreading throughout her body. The words are like the lashes of a whip. *What's that horrible bellowing?* she thinks, startled. *Why is this man yelling at me? What did I do wrong?* She feels completely bewildered, and the lovely scene that surrounds her doesn't match the inner uproar at all.

Then, to her astonishment, she hears the word "Brittany" again and again. *Why is this bellowing man calling me Brittany? It just doesn't make sense,* Molly thinks, perplexed. But then she realizes that the man doesn't mean her at all but seems instead to be aiming his words at Brittany, who just now was in her thoughts.

Inside herself, Molly is knitting her brow. She's no longer sure if this really is her own inside. After all, she did get to know her inner world, and it was quite different from what she's seeing now. Something is not quite right here.

Slowly, it dawns on her: this is not her body at all, and instead she's sensing what it feels like inside Brittany's body! Wasn't she just thinking how she wished she could put herself in other people's shoes? And no sooner had she wished it than it happened. *Great,* she thinks to herself, *now I've gone and done it! I really should be a little more careful about what I wish for.* Because is that really what she wants now—to feel the same as what Brittany is feeling?

The whole thing is kind of eerie, and Molly makes up her mind to not stay here too much longer. If she could wish herself into someone else, then shouldn't she be able to wish herself out? But... now that she's already here, her curiosity gets the better of her. And she decides to stick around a little longer and keep listening, no matter how much the uproar upsets her.

The more Molly hears, the more obvious it becomes that Brittany's father is doing the yelling and never seems to stop. However curious Molly may have been, the din is really unbearable! She tries to escape the aggressive voice by crawling more and more into the body. There has to be a safe space somewhere! But the noise seems to be everywhere—there's simply no escape.

Just as with the journey inside her own body, Molly

is right in the thick of it here. But while her own body looked like a perfectly organized laboratory that functioned with the harmony of a flawlessly synchronized orchestra, with Brittany, nothing seems to fit. It's as if all the instruments are playing wildly and uncontrollably, with the whole thing underscored by her father's roaring. Everything seems loud and discordant.

Molly covers her ears, but that doesn't help, since all it does is to block the sounds from outside. Inside, however, it stays the same, and there's no escaping this body.

Luckily, she remembers that her guardian angel is always by her side. "What's going on here?" she frantically calls out to him. "Why is it such a mess here? How can Brittany live like this? It's almost unbearable!"

"I know, my dear Molly," her guardian angel immediately replies, and although he speaks softly, the noise luckily doesn't stand a chance against his gentle yet surprisingly penetrating voice. "As you can hear, Brittany grew up with a very short-tempered father who was also very demanding. His words and expectations are all she can perceive. She's never known anything else. Even when he's not there, his voice and his demands still echo inside her. Rarely does anything else get through to her. It places her under enormous stress."

"That's awful! What can we do about it?" Molly asks, horrified.

"I think you know what you can do," her guardian angel replies gently. "You weren't feeling so well yourself a few weeks ago. What helped you?"

Molly thinks it over. "I realized that my innermost core is love, and that was an incredibly beautiful experience." She has to smile now, even over the noise.

Her guardian angel also appears to be smiling as he asks, "So what would you wish for Brittany?"

Molly answers without having to give it one more thought. "That's easy—just that she recognizes who she really is, that she knows that the noise is not the truth. That's what I wish for Brittany!"

"Hmmm, Molly, I have to admit that's the nicest wish you could have for another person. But how are you going to do that? You can't exactly explain it to her, can you? She doesn't even know you're inside her, so to speak, and aside from that, she knows hardly anything other than this noise. Which means that she thinks it's the truth. You'll have a hard time fighting that with words alone, don't you think?"

Molly nods. "Yes, I guess that's true," she admits. She's feeling somewhat helpless. Isn't there anything she can do?

Her guardian angel encourages her: "Don't give up just yet, Molly. Maybe there's something you can do, after all. Think about it: before you realized that you were pure love in your innermost core, back when you thought you were just a girl with no special abilities, what did you do to transform the things inside you?"

Molly is thinking. She doesn't want to make a mistake—this is too important. If she can help Brittany to free herself of her burden, then she definitely wants to do it. She thinks back to her journey into her inner world: the landscape with the gray mountain, the hunched figures, the slimy frogs... they all came across as ugly, dark, and dead-looking. And then she did something that suddenly made them beautiful, peaceful, and alive. But what was that exactly? Maybe she could do the same thing for Brittany. Molly's wondrous journey is going through her mind again—the encounter with all those feelings and sensations that she didn't want to acknowledge at first but then grew to like, after all.

"I started to feel compassion for them," she finally says, beaming with relief. "At first, I found them revolting, and I was afraid. But when I looked more closely, I felt sort of sorry for them and realized they weren't as scary as I first thought. In fact, they were almost more insecure than I was. That's why I didn't want to run from them anymore—I wanted to help them instead. I literally opened my heart to them. I remember how it kept growing bigger and bigger inside me. I could actually feel it. The funny thing is that, through that, the beings transformed and suddenly became beautiful.

But you know all this—you were there yourself. That was all inside me, though, so of course I could influence what went on. But Brittany is a separate person. There's no way I can change her. I don't know how you can compare the two!"

"You remembered it well, Molly," the guardian angel says in a kindly tone. "But let's take a closer look at the whole thing. When you open your heart to other people or even to things and you develop compassion for them, it's almost as if you can feel their pain and joy yourself, isn't it?"

"Yes, with people, anyway," Molly replies. She remembers one girl in her class who got so nervous when the teacher called on her that her brain seemed to freeze, and she couldn't answer the simplest questions. She was an intelligent girl, just nervous. And every time it was this girl's turn, Molly would feel like she was living through it herself and her throat would tighten as well. So she had compassion for people in any case. But her guardian angel also mentioned things, although this made no sense to Molly because things are not alive.

As usual, her guardian angel could read her mind.

"Think about it, we can have compassion for more than just people. You even had it for your feelings."

True, thinks Molly, *how could I forget that so quickly?*

The voice continues: "And as a child, you felt hurt

when you thought your doll or your teddy bear had hurt themselves. They're not people, either, but they meant just as much to you. Many people have compassion for nature, for trees and flowers, and there's a huge number of people that find it easier to feel compassion for animals than for their fellow human beings. What I'm saying is that you can feel compassion not just for other people but for everything in this world."

Molly nods eagerly. *Yes, that's true,* she thinks. When she sees animals being tortured on TV, it always hurts her, too. She can hardly watch, and luckily her mother quickly changes the channel.

Her guardian angel prompts her: "Let's pursue this thought a little more. This is important. It will help you not only to see the world differently but to transform it, to enchant it. You have more power than you think, Molly."

Molly is excited. She feels big and important. "Okay, then let's get started," she says eagerly.

"I'm sure you remember the voice of Love, Molly. Do you remember what it said to you?"

"I'll never forget it! It said that in our innermost core all of us are love, that love is eternal, that everything comes from it and everything will find its way back," Molly answers, her cheeks glowing with excitement. Her encounter with Love was the most beautiful thing that had ever happened to her.

"Exactly," her guardian angel replies with a smile.

"Everything, absolutely everything, comes from Love, which means that in their origin, all things are one. Behind all the differences we see on the surface, everything springs from a single energy. When you feel compassion for another being, you dissolve the superficial boundaries between you and the other, and more and more, you feel the oneness that exists between you. You feel the other's pain as your own pain, the other's joy as your own joy. If you were to go deeper and deeper, everything else would dissolve in the Source, and Love would be all that remains as the one unifying energy. That, then, is absolute bliss. So when you say to someone, 'I love you,' what you're really saying is, 'With you, it's easy for me to experience the oneness called love.' With some people it's easy, and with others it's just difficult. But the unity of all beings is always there—it's just that we often forget this."

"Yeah, okay," Molly answers, "but how do I use that to help Brittany?" As great as this conversation may be, Molly is starting to get impatient.

Her guardian angel comes to her aid again: "We're getting to that now, Molly. Love would be worthless if it were nothing more than an abstract concept with no practical value. But it's the greatest power there is— actually, the only power. That means that if you let the love well up inside you so that you're so filled with it that it flows out to other people as well, then people can't help but be filled with that love through and through and transformed from the inside out."

Molly looks puzzled.

Her guardian angel continues: "Let me make it a little more vivid for you:"

Imagine you're a deep well. Below you is the groundwater. It's everywhere, and everyone needs it to live. But not everyone can access the groundwater, and many have forgotten that groundwater even exists. The land around you is dry and parched. You, however, reach so deep into the earth that the water has a chance to come up. Oh, what am I saying? It has no other way of rising up except through you. You don't have to do anything—just be ready for the water to push its way up from below. And so, you let the water fill you up, all the way up to the rim and over so that the water flows out and onto the rest of the land, moistening and saturating it. Through you, more and more water rises up and flows out, and now the land around you becomes fruitful again. The flowers begin to bloom, some more quickly, some more slowly. But the water will ceaselessly saturate all things, and all will drink in this vital elixir of life."

A single well is enough to accomplish this. And then maybe a second well would be added and a third, and in a short time, everything will be blooming and fragrant and filled with life. The plants will recover and remember once more that groundwater does, in fact, exist, and they will seek it out themselves. Then their roots will grow deep enough to nourish themselves from the groundwater. And maybe one day the rain will return to roam across the land again, bringing the needed moisture in abundance. Rivers will form, and at some point, no one will even think of the time when people believed there was not enough water for all. Then they may no longer need the wells. But until that happens, although the water is actually available to all, they will need them to retrieve it and bring it into the world."

Be such a well, Molly, not for water but for love, which is even more important than water. Because unlike water and all other things, love is infinite. It never runs low, no matter how much you give away! And at the same time, you can never give too much, because love likes nothing better than to be given away. Give love to the people and things around you until they themselves remember that love is their essence as well and they begin to seek it in themselves. That's all you need to do, Molly, if you want to make the world a better place. You can't change everything outwardly, and you don't need to. It's enough to remind people of their true essence. Every child and every adult can do this, which means that all of us have the power to transform the world."

Molly's eyes are shining as she listens. "I see," she now says. "And you're right. When I feel Brittany's pain, it really hurts me, too, and I can't help but open my heart to her. I had no idea what she had to live with!"

And with these words, Molly opens her heart even wider and feels the love rising up within her, literally surging upwards and flowing towards Brittany. The more the love touches Brittany, encircling and lapping against her, the quieter the noise in her body becomes. The love seems to simply dissolve the noise—without struggle or effort. Now, Molly is slowly noticing other sounds, sweet tones that rise up out of the silence, at first subdued, then ever more spirited until they finally fill the room with their tender, delicate melody. What before had sounded like loud drumming was probably Brittany's wildly pounding heart, which was now giving way to a soothingly steady beat. Molly also believes she can make out the mesmerizing tones of a flute, and if she's not mistaken, she could swear she can also discern the soft sounds of a violin as they ripple outward in gentle waves. More and more, Brittany's body is beginning to resemble a harmonious symphony orchestra. *Just as it was probably meant to be,* thinks Molly as she enjoys the beautiful melody.

Now that the noise has died down, Molly can also hear the father's words more clearly:

"Brittany, have you done your homework yet? You know that you need to study."

Oddly enough, Molly no longer hears the aggression in his voice. Instead, she mostly notices the father's fear and uncertainty. And for the first time, Brittany hears this, too, so now she asks her father in a soft voice:

"Papa, what's going on with you? You're so incredibly quick-tempered, and you never seem happy with what I do. I don't think you have any idea how hard that is on me. I feel like I'll never be able to please you. Can't we just talk normally?"

Molly can now see the father in her mind's eye, and she notices that he's looking at his daughter in amazement. Brittany has never spoken like this before, openly asking him what's going on. Usually, it's just one big bout of trading blows. And while her father doesn't normally tolerate backtalk and scolds Brittany for being impudent, to his own astonishment, he now hears himself answering honestly:

"It's all the worries I have, Brittany—I'm just in over my head sometimes. But there's no use talking about it now. You wouldn't understand."

"Maybe I would," Brittany protests, challenging him. "At least, give it a try."

"Okay," her father hesitates but gives in, "if you absolutely want to. So, Brittany, my job just isn't secure. People are being laid off on a daily basis, and while I'm doing my best, I can never be sure that it won't be my turn at some point."

Am I really talking like this to my daughter right now? he wonders.

But before he can change his mind, the words keep pouring out of him:

"And if I lose my job, I don't know how I'm going to pay for all this: the apartment, your hobbies, our whole life. Sometimes, it's all simply too much—all the responsibility. And that's why it's important that you study hard so you can have a better job than I do and you don't have to worry about it."

Brittany is feeling completely different from before. She doesn't know where it came from, but she's suddenly sensing a peace she never knew before, and it's making room for a new feeling of optimism. She's also grateful for the honest exchange with her father. And from her, too, the words are now spilling out by themselves:

"I do understand you, Papa. At least, I think I do. But you know, it doesn't help when we treat each other the way we have been lately. Because that just makes our lives a living hell even before anything bad has happened, doesn't it? Can't we try to have faith instead that everything will be okay? Until now, everything has felt incredibly cold and cramped. But I don't think that's how our lives were meant to be. Why don't we try to enjoy the moment and be there for each other? And if things get harder, we'll manage. We'll come up with something then. But for now, we can just enjoy life, can't we?"

Brittany's father has tears in his eyes. He's not used to showing his feelings or having conversations of this sort. Not even with his wife, much less his daughter. He finds it a bit embarrassing to talk so openly about his feelings and thoughts, but just like Brittany, he feels different deep down inside—brighter somehow, and a new feeling of optimism is growing within him, too. So far, he's always been able to manage. And if he does lose his job, he'll be able to deal with that, too—with the loving support of his family, who really just want to be happy and who will always have his back, whether he's successful or not.

Then, on a sudden impulse, he takes Brittany in his arms and holds her tightly as the tears run down both their cheeks. They feel an old, familiar love, though one that was never recognized, now rising up within them and flowing from heart to heart. And everything around them is opening up, expanding, becoming brighter. Suddenly, the father has to smile at his own fear. He was willing to ruin his life for a feeling? Even though, so far, nothing had actually happened?

And then he makes up his mind that tomorrow he'll go see his boss and ask him to clarify things. It's better to look things in the face than to crawl into your shell and spend your days hoping your worst fears won't come true. And if he really does lose his job, he's sure his boss will give him a letter of recommendation. *I'll deal with that when the time comes,* he thinks. *One thing at a time.* And in the truest sense of the word, he can feel how a weight has been lifted from his heart.

Molly is watching the scene, and the tears are running down her cheeks, too. Once again, she feels moved by the power of love. In a matter of minutes, Brittany's home and body have both been transformed from a madhouse into a place of optimism and warmth. Molly has to smile through her tears. She could actually feel what it felt like inside another person's body. She thinks back to the journey inside her own body and how there were minor blockages there as well, but those were nothing compared with what was going on inside Brittany.

Molly is glad that Brittany is also now at peace, and she turns away from her and back to her spot by the stream. Then she takes a deep breath, and full of joy and lightness, she shines her love upon the bees and flowers and even upon her bicycle, which she can always count on to transport her around the area. She feels love for everything around her, and everything seems to turn a little brighter, happier, more alive. *So this is how life is meant to be,* Molly thinks to herself. *Yes, this feels right.*

And so, Molly simply sits there for a while, enjoying her existence and absorbing what she just experienced. Her thoughts then slowly wander to her teacher, Mr. Baker . She doesn't know why she feels the need to think of him just now. Maybe because Brittany bullied him, too. But if Molly is honest with herself, she has to admit she was never especially nice to him, either. His teaching is just so incredibly dull, and he can't assert himself, so everyone does whatever they want with him.

No sooner has she finished this thought than Molly finds herself in a misty, black-and-white landscape. She shudders. Where has she landed now? This day is full of lots of strange surprises! She looks around and realizes with astonishment that it looks basically the same as her own emotional landscape. But while her landscape is bubbling with life and a land inhabited by fairies, gnomes, and butterflies, where the sun is shining and the water in the rivers flows gold, here everything is gray and drab. No color or sound pierces the dull monotony. Molly shivers. Where on earth has she landed?

"Rather dreary here, isn't it, Molly?" Her guardian angel comes to the rescue. "And no wonder, because you're now in the emotional world of your—oh, so dull —teacher, Mr. Baker ," he teases.

Molly rolls her eyes. From Brittany's body to Mr. Baker 's boring emotional landscape.... Is this really necessary? Her guardian angel took her words way too seriously!

And Molly does, in fact, now see Mr. Baker sitting sadly at home by his table, listlessly staring at a candle. He is thinking of his wife, who passed away last year, and how he misses her so. Since she's been gone, he no longer has any idea why he's even alive. She was his whole world, the only one who ever truly listened to him and took him seriously. She also made him laugh, and every time she laughed, Mr. Baker felt as though the sun was rising and warming his heart. Now he had no one left.

Sometimes, he pretends she's still there, and that gives him a momentary feeling of comfort. But when he remembers that she's really gone, he feels like his heart is being ripped from his chest, and the pain is sometimes so intense he can hardly bear it. Other times, he's not even sure he has a heart anymore. Then, everything inside and around him is dull, like now, and he wonders what he's living for. He seems to no longer have any passion for anything—everything is so meaningless.

At least, he used to enjoy his work. As a young teacher, he would leap out of bed every morning, full of pep, and look forward to the day ahead. He made diligent preparations to give his best to the children and make the topic as understandable as possible. But he soon realized that he lacked the kind of personality that others valued. He wasn't funny or entertaining, and the children found his slow, deliberate manner utterly boring. That girl Brittany, in particular, was always trying to turn his life into total hell, and he felt ashamed that he feared the sharp tongue of a schoolgirl.

MOLLY IS SITTING on the grass and can feel her teacher's emotions almost as if they were her own. She now also senses why his landscape is so gray: there's no longer any joy there, no vitality. He has allowed the gray veil of grief to cover everything without giving the other feelings a chance to grow. His joy and vitality were literally being smothered.

The tears are running down Molly's cheeks once more, and she feels a deep sense of compassion for her teacher. Now she lets her love flow towards him, too, because he seems to have forgotten the love that exists within him. And as if by some miracle, this tickles awake the love inside him, which was merely waiting to be summoned again. And just as before, when love had simply dissolved the noise inside Brittany, it now makes colorful butterflies mount up to the skies, where they easily lift the veil and bear it away on their wings.

Molly is watching the action, her mouth agape. Without the gray mist, she has a clear view of the entire landscape. Now she can also see the grief itself in its various elflike forms, and she watches, moved, as it solemnly strides away.

To Molly, sorrow is now like a good, old friend, and she sees that it's visibly relieved to be allowed to withdraw. For although it exists as a natural part of this varied inner world, it never saw any value in taking over the entire emotional landscape. That was too much to bear, and it's glad to be allowed to resume its usual place.

Molly can see that the mournful figures have a little figure of fear in their midst, who now turns to Molly and waves affectionately. Molly waves back. Fear is something she also remembers well—and, yes, there's still some there since Molly is, after all, a human being, and every living creature is familiar with fear. Now, though, it's just a little part of her that peeks out curiously once in a while, and then that's all. Besides, Molly has grown to love it, with its tender vulnerability.

But now she's enjoying the wonderful spectacle unfolding before her eyes: without the dreary veil, the landscape is open once more to the sun and its magical light play. Faint at first but growing stronger, it sends down its rays, warming the land and bathing it in a golden glow. Attracted by the glow and the dance of the butterflies, the first gnomes poke their noses out of their houses now, amazed at how the landscape is slowly coming to life again. A smile appears upon their faces—at first, timid, then growing wider and wider until they finally dare to go outside. They hesitate, but then, more and more assured, they doff their hats and eagerly set about tending the gardens, creating space for new and colorful flowers. They have been waiting for this day for a very long time!

In the background, Molly now also sees the frogs and dragons, which she knows from her own emotional world. She bursts out laughing in amazement: everyone's emotional life seems basically the same! Sure, it's all there to different degrees, but the similarities are unmistakable: sorrow, joy, fear, and shame—they're there in all of us.

To Molly's delight, the fairies are now flying in and lighting up the sky with their glittery dresses. They're weaving rivers with their golden hair, so Molly decides to look in on Mr. Baker to see how he's doing in his room. He's still sitting at his table looking at the candle, but slowly he notices how something is relaxing inside him. Somehow, a quiet joy seems to be rising up within him, even though he had no idea he still had it. He wants to hold on to this joy, but he senses that something is keeping him back. He has a feeling he knows what it is, which is why he now thinks of his deceased wife and speaks into the room:

"Isabelle, please give me a sign that you're here and that it's okay for me to feel good again. I'm realizing now," he says, astonished at himself, "that I didn't dare allow myself to be happy. When you were suffering so during your illness and then died from it, I felt like a failure. I couldn't take away your pain, and I couldn't keep back death. I felt like I should have died with you. I felt downright guilty that I was still alive. But this needs to end now, Isabelle. I am alive, and I'm still relatively young and healthy. And I have a job that I'm sure could be fun again if I just let it. The children at the school need me, and even if they're difficult sometimes, each and every one of them deserves that I give them my best. I owe it to myself as well. And so, Isabelle, my love, I'm now going to start to live again. But I would still love to have a sign from you, because I still love you and will always feel connected to you. It would be nice to know that you're there for me."

He feels a little silly as he speaks these words alone in the room by himself, and he doesn't actually expect a response. But all of a sudden, he feels a glow rising up within him, and it seems to fill not only him but the whole room with brightness. Amazed, he looks at the candle to see if it's the source of this sudden display, but it just keeps flickering softly. No, the glow is indeed coming from inside himself. It's as though a veil has been pulled away and Isabelle's smile is rising up out of him like the sun to make everything in and around him shine.

And, yes, Mr. Baker is beaming now. For he sees with absolute clarity that, whatever the outward conditions, the love that was so fulfilling between him and his wife can never die—and that Isabelle does not begrudge him his happiness but even wishes it for him with all her heart.

A long forgotten love of life awakens within him, and Molly watches with a smile as Mr. Baker gets up from his seat with gusto, turns on some fun dance music, and laughs as he spins around. Afterwards, he takes a long bath, gives himself a good shave, and resolves to go into town tomorrow to buy some new clothes. He has let himself go long enough, and that's over now! And maybe he'll even take the pretty German teacher out to dinner. Isabelle would surely be happy for him to have that as well. And with that, he lights up once again, and the glow is especially bright.

Molly opens her eyes and takes a deep breath. Whew! What an experience! She, too, feels like a veil has been pulled away from her eyes. She had always found her teacher a rather strange character. At best, she was indifferent to him, and she could never imagine that he had feelings as well. In reality, though, his emotional world is even similar to hers. That immediately makes him much more likeable to Molly, and she knows that from now on, she will see him with totally different eyes.

Molly almost feels a bit exhausted. All these emotions and new discoveries are, after all, quite a lot for one day! But she's sensing... that there's one more person she would like to get to know a little better. A person she takes for granted but who is always there for her and puts everything on the back burner when it comes to her, Molly: her mother! Her mother always tries her best to understand Molly, and now Molly also wants to take a peek into her mother's life to find out if she knows her mother as well as she thinks she does. Molly is a little nervous. She's not sure if she has the right to look inside her mother's inner world. She almost feels like she's snooping around in secret.

"What do you think, guardian angel, am I even allowed to do all that? First Brittany's body, then Mr. Baker 's feelings, and now Mama, too. Am I maybe a little too curious, after all?" she asks him in her mind.

"Don't worry, Molly," comes the prompt reply from her guardian angel. "Love would never let you see the parts of someone's life that they want to keep secret. All you can see is what other people want to share and where they're looking for advice and help, even when this yearning is hidden deep within their hearts. Every person longs to be seen and understood, and compassion means being able to put yourself in other people's shoes—but obviously only to the extent that they allow it."

And so, Molly closes her eyes in joyful anticipation, her heart pounding slightly as she puts herself in her mother's place. But instead of feeling joy, what she sees makes her sad. As expected, her mother has a beautiful emotional landscape inside her, dominated mostly by graceful fairies—and cheerful gnomes, of course. That comes as no surprise to Molly. Her mother always has a smile in her eyes, and she's the most graceful woman Molly knows. And fairies, as she recalls, are the symbol of grace. But what Molly also sees is her mother's mind, that fascinating world that she, Molly, lit up with fireworks when she saw herself on stage as a successful singer. And then she remembers a couple of dark clouds that came from her untrue and diminishing thoughts—for example, that nothing in life is a gift. Through that experience, Molly learned that life is one big gift. But with her mother, she now sees only a couple of scattered firework sparks. Mostly, it's just dark, low-hanging clouds. Molly grows sad. How can this be? Why does her wonderful, perpetually positive mother have such a dreary mind?

Molly listens more closely and now hears scattered snippets of thought. The words "duty," "humility," and "family" come up again and again. Molly is startled. Can it be that her mother regrets having her and her brother? But no, what she reads in her mother's thoughts instead is that she, too, was once a girl with dreams and needs. And they were especially strong when her mother was young and had her whole life before her. But then she got married, had children, and began to put her own needs aside to meet the needs of her family. Over time, it was the proverbial tale of her own dreams crumbling under the weight of duty.

Molly can't help herself: she opens her heart more and more towards her mother, sending her endless love. And as the love flows out to her mother, her mind grows lighter and lighter, and the dark clouds lift. The old dreams that were buried for so long are now coming forward, hesitantly at first, as new life is breathed into them. The dreams are taking shape, and Molly is amazed to find that her mother always wanted to be a painter. She sees the beautiful images that used to form in her mother's imagination and were forever waiting to be put on canvas. But they never made it there, for the sense of duty had held them captive. Now they were blooming again in her mother's mind in the loveliest hues—colorful, happy pictures, full of flowers in lush nature. Her mother is like a never-ending palette of colors.

Molly is so moved that her tears begin to flow. She had no idea her mother had such vitality and creativity. And she feels the need to bring out this beauty so it can be shared with others. Inspired by this urgent energy, real fireworks now also appear in her mother as they constantly form new flowers and landscapes.

As much as Molly has always admired her mother, she would never have guessed her to be the creator of such a rich world!

In time, she sees more and more of her mother's desires blaze up—it seems to never end: there are trips, many trips to southern countries full of lightness and a zest for life. Travel to Italy, above all, appears again and again. Her mother seems to receive her inspiration from this beautiful land, but it's been a long time since she was last there. And there's still so much there that she hasn't yet seen. She has never been to Rome or Florence, and the yearning for these cities bubbles up within her and shoots up like fireworks. These cities then make way for other places, other dreams, hopes, and desires. Molly watches the fiery magic a while longer and then decides she's seen enough. It's time to leave her mother to her own world of thoughts.

MOLLY OPENS her eyes and sits up. She is exhausted but happy. Three journeys to three people: one to the body of someone she rather disliked, then to the emotional landscape of someone she didn't particularly care about, and finally to the mental world of her own mother, whom she had naturally always loved but hadn't known as well as she thought. And every single time, love changed everything for the better, breathing color and brightness into even the most hopeless situation. It truly has the power to transform all things, bringing light and life where darkness or wasteland existed before.

Molly sits there a while longer, listening to the sounds of nature all around her—the stream, the birds, the buzzing bees, and her own heartbeat as well. She feels a deep sense of peace.

Then she gets on her bike once more and slowly rides back home. That evening, she is very quiet. She first needs to process the impressive experiences of the day, and she goes to bed early. *No more wild dreams tonight, dear guardian angel,* she thinks to herself. *I've really had enough for one day.* And with that, she falls into a deep sleep.

Whe Molly awakens the next morning, the events of the previous day immediately pop into her head. Everything seems so unreal to her now. *Did that actually happen yesterday,* she wonders, *or was it just my imagination going crazy?* She's not sure. Even on the way to school, she can't stop thinking about the day before. It all felt so real! Had anything actually changed in the people she visited yesterday in such an unusual way? *No, I'm sure I was just imagining things,* she concludes matter-of-factly. Now it's back to reality, and she's about to have a geography lesson with sad, old Mr. Baker .

Except that when she arrives at the school, Mr. Baker doesn't look sad at all. He's laughing and full of pep. Molly could swear she's never seen him laugh before! And on top of that, he looks completely different... younger, much younger. And he's cracking jokes —that's something totally new!

"Good morning, children," he says in the best of moods, and the whole class stares at him, mesmerized. "Today is such a beautiful day—let's not stay stuck inside this school building. Nature is waiting for us to explore it firsthand. We want to feel, smell, touch, and sense that we're a part of it as well. So come on, kids, let's go outside!"

The class can hardly believe their eyes and ears. What ever happened to their boring, perpetually somewhat sad teacher? But now is not the time to think about that. The offer to get out of the school building is far too appealing for that, and they run outside before he has a chance to change his mind.

But he doesn't. Instead, he tramps along beside them through the forest and fields, and his momentum is so infectious that soon a whole throng of students has gathered around him and is listening to his words.

Molly stays somewhat behind and watches what's happening with interest. Suddenly, Brittany approaches her. *Oh no, does this have to be now? Everything is so nice right now.* Even if she does understand Brittany better now, she really doesn't need anyone making fun of her and provoking her at the moment. But then she notices that Brittany looks different, too.

"Hi, Molly," she says, looking down at the ground. "I brought you something." And then she gives Molly a small bag of cookies. "I made them myself," she mumbles.

Now Molly's eyes are practically popping out of her head. "Thanks," she replies uncertainly. "But why are you bringing me cookies?"

"I'm not really sure myself," Brittany answers. "It just came over me. But I was also kind of mean to you a lot of the time. To you and to other people as well. I'm sorry for that. I don't want that anymore. Do you think we could put that behind us?"

"Already forgotten." Molly smiles and can feel her heart jumping for joy. Then she and Brittany stroll side by side down the pathway, talking shyly at first and then more and more excitedly about God and the world. Molly realizes with amazement that behind Brittany's tough facade is a sensitive and intelligent girl, and she resolves to nurture the tender shoot of friendship that has just begun to blossom between them.

Molly is beaming all over as she makes her way

home. How fascinated she was a few weeks ago to learn that she is the queen of her body, her feelings, and her thoughts. But now she sees that through her love alone, she can enchant not only herself but the whole world! She has much more power than she thought.

BUT NOW SHE'S even more amazed on coming home to see how festively her mother has set the table on the terrace, with cheerful Italian music resounding throughout the house! Her mother has poured lemonade and set all sorts of delicious tidbits on the table. When Molly comes in, her mother gives her a happy, affectionate hug.

"Come, Molly, what do you say we forget about your homework for now and enjoy the afternoon?"

Molly beams.

"You know, Molly, we have such a nice life, but we rarely enjoy it, and it's been a long time since we've really had a chat. Your brother is at a friend's today, and Papa is working. Which means that the two of us have plenty of time together, and I want to hear how you're doing. But first, I have a present for you."

And with that, she hands Molly an envelope. Molly is dumbfounded. A present for her—just like that? As she opens the envelope, she finds a gift certificate for singing lessons! She can hardly believe her eyes. Until now, her mother never supported her big dream of learning to sing.

"Molly, my love, I blame myself so much. I know, after all, how much you love to sing, and I never really took it seriously. I wanted you to focus on other things, to do your homework so that later on you could have a solid career with a steady income. I imagined you becoming a lawyer or a doctor, for example. I very nearly laughed at your dream of becoming a singer, even though I know you have talent and you enjoy it so much. But now all I want is for you to be happy. Of course, you should keep doing your homework, but take a few singing lessons to see if you really enjoy it. And if that's what you want to do, then Papa and I will support you with all our hearts. We talked about it yesterday, and we've agreed. And we also think your brother should become a firefighter, if that's what he wants," she adds, laughing.

Molly laughs along with her.

"And there's something else I wanted to tell you, Molly," her mother continues, blushing slightly. "I have dreams, too, although I'd almost forgotten about them. And the biggest of those dreams is to paint. That's why I've now signed up for a painting class. It feels like the most selfish thing I've done in a long time, but it's also one of the most beautiful," she says with a sparkle that reminds Molly of the photos from her mother's youth. "I've been looking forward to it all day like a little kid.

Yes, like a child...." she adds with a thoughtful look. "You children still know how to be happy. Unlike us adults, who have almost forgotten. I could still learn a lot from you, Molly!"

Molly and her mother are both beaming from ear to ear. Then Molly says with a wink, "You know what, Mama, I've also had an idea. Why don't the two of us go on a trip somewhere once in a while? Maybe this year, we could go to Florence. And next year to Rome."

Her mother looks at her, stunned. "What a lovely idea!" she exclaims. "Florence and Rome—I've always wanted to go there. It's as if you read my mind. That's almost like magic."

She gives Molly an odd look. Her daughter has certainly changed a lot in the past few weeks. Not only has she developed an entirely new self-confidence and natural composure, but she also radiates a kind of wisdom. And somehow this development seems to have an impact on everyone around Molly. Everything around her is changing for the better, including herself, Molly's mother.

But before she can say anything more, Molly starts to laugh. "Magic... Florence and Rome, Mama, that's obvious. So many great operas come from Italy, and both cities will be a great destination when I start my singing lessons. And they go with painting as well, so we can both be inspired."

Ah, so that's it, thinks her mother, relieved by this

explanation. *Mothers and daughters are, after all, a lot more alike than people think.*

And then they sit down, and the mother asks Molly:

"So, Molly, what's new in your life?"

"Oh, not much," Molly answers, not quite truthfully, and then thinks to herself: *Sorry, Love, but it's probably a little too soon for me to talk about you. One thing at a time.*

And then she tells her mother about the miraculous changes that have taken place in Brittany and her teacher—and for which she has absolutely no explanation at all....

And Love smiles.

DID YOU LIKE THE STORY?

We sincerely hope you enjoyed MOLLY ENCHANTS HER WORLD! If you did, you will also love the next story in the series:

MOLLY, ARCHITECT OF LIFE

After her extraordinary journeys, Molly now knows about her inner life and the inner lives of others. But she wouldn't be Molly if a new question wasn't gnawing at her: is her guardian angel right when he claims she can create exactly the life she wants? And is it really as easy as child's play, as he says? Molly has her doubts, but she sets out to find out!

ABOUT THE AUTHOR

Anna Camilla Kupka grew up in Düsseldorf/Germany, where she first studied law and then earned her doctorate at the University of Münster. She subsequently attended the Stanford Graduate School of Business in California/USA and lived in Dublin/Ireland for a long time. Today, Anna lives and loves in Zurich/Switzerland. She believes that happiness is our birthright, and she is especially committed to helping young people recognize and live their full potential.

Printed in Great Britain
by Amazon

11633111R00027